This book is full of blank pages.
Despite years of research,
I was unable to find anything beneficial
to state on this subject,
so please feel free
to use this book for notes.